12-10-16

MW01613855

Extreme Makeover

ROGER DERKSEN
609 W 96TH TERRACE
KANSAS CITY, MO 64114
rogermwd@outlook.com
816-520-7414

Extreme Makeover

Spiritual Edition

Roger Derksen

© 2016 Roger Derksen
All rights reserved.

ISBN: 1530499801
ISBN 13: 9781530499809

TABLE OF CONTENTS

INTRODUCTION

Jeremiah 33:3 says, "Call unto me, and I will answer thee, and show thee great and mighty things, which thou knowest not." James 1:5 says, "If any of you lack wisdom, let him ask of God, that giveth to all men liberally, and upbraideth not; and it shall be given him." God has great things in store for us. Sometimes things may be beyond our imagination. God does want us to prosper, but he wants us to follow his plan, and he wants the credit. God has a plan for our lives, but we have to read the manual to learn that plan. As I was writing this book, I realized I was writing it to myself. I was frustrated with the way things where going in my life, but knowing there was more to the Bible than I was tapping into, I began to look for answers, and I discovered the Bible is the best place to find them.

My gifting is teaching, and that makes studying the Bible much easier to do. Your gifting may be different, and you may find it hard to spend much time studying, but you must find a way to feed on the Word of God and allow him to guide you. There is no set way to do this. Find a way that works for you.

QUESTIONS

"What is God's will for my life?" "How do I know what God wants me to do?" "Why doesn't God talk to me?" "Why is it I can't seem to get victory?" We could go on and on with questions and wonder why we struggle. I grew up in the church. When I was born, my dad was a preacher. I was taught the usual Bible stories and probably gave my heart to the Lord more than once. But it's hard to get victory when you depend on the faith of other people.

I had to study the Word for myself; I had to "hide it in my heart" (Ps 119:11) and appropriate it in my life. I had to see and experience for myself that God is who and what he said he is. I used to wonder why God never talked to me, until I realized it was I who was not listening. Listening to God starts by studying his Word. Romans 10:17 says, "Faith cometh by hearing and hearing by the word of God." We have to know what God's Word says so that we are not misled by smooth- or fast-talking people or by false doctrine.

Sometimes we have to lay aside our religious teachings, traditions, and preconceived notions and let God show us what his Word really means. A word of caution, though: the Word will shake up your theology. I don't want to be too hard on my childhood teachers. They were well-meaning people who taught what they believed. With today's study aids, it is much easier to study the Bible for ourselves. Sometimes what we learn does not line up with what we were taught.

We do need people to go to sometimes to be sure we are correct—pastors, teachers, or other people we trust. But we must follow scripture and God's leading, not well-meaning people or past teachings.

What is theology? Theology is simply the study of God. We all have preconceived notions and ideas about who and what God is. Getting into the Word of God may show us that some of those teachings may not be quite right. But God is faithful, and his Word will not lead us astray.

We need to use the talents God has given us and not try to develop our own. What would we do if we knew we could not fail? That may very well be what God has called us to do. It is an inward longing that won't go away. We generally think of a talented person as someone who can sing, preach, or teach or maybe someone who is a great leader. There are other talents such as serving or giving (not necessarily money—maybe of your time). Maybe you are to be an automotive mechanic or a truck driver. What is your heart's desire? Maybe that is what God called you to do. God has given us talents to use for his honor and glory. We need to develop the plans that God has given us and not try to develop our own. Don't allow someone to talk you into something you don't feel right about. That may be their dream but not yours. We can accomplish tremendous things when we set our hearts and minds to them, but that might not be what God wants us to do. We will not be truly happy or content unless we are in the will of God. To find true contentment, we need to be in the will of God. Anything that takes us away from the will of God will separate us from God and hinder his ability to work in our lives.

GOD HAS MORE

God has much more in store for us than we are receiving. We are not receiving because we don't understand the contract. That's right. God's Word is a contract. In the Bible it is called a blood covenant. A blood covenant was an agreement between two people sealed in blood, and it was binding unto death in that culture. In that culture, if I made a blood covenant with someone and then broke that covenant, my own family members would seek me out and kill me. The Bible, or contract, is full of things God will do for us, but we must fulfill our end of the contract. How can we keep our end of the contract if we don't know what the terms are? The terms are written in the Word of God.

Too often we make our plans and want God to bless them. Guess what? That doesn't work. Contrary to what we want to believe, God is smarter than we are. We will have to do things his way to receive his blessings. Exodus 15:26 says, "If thou wilt diligently hearken to the voice of the Lord thy God, and wilt do that which is right in his sight, and wilt give ear to his commandments, and keep all his statues, I will put none of these diseases upon thee, which I have brought upon the Egyptians: for I am the Lord that healeth thee." God promised the Israelites in the desert that he would take care of them if they would follow him, but they had to do as God would direct them. If they did not follow God, then he could not help them. The same is true with us. If we follow God's leading, then he will be able to pour out his blessing upon us. If we don't follow God, then there isn't much he can do for us. God is a covenant God. We have to do our part, and then he will do his part. If, as a child, I did as I was told, my dad was much more willing to help me. If I was disobedient, then I would face punishment in some way. The same is true with God. If we are obedient, then he will help us. God does not give us sickness, disease, or sorrow, but he will not help us because we have broken the covenant.

GOD HAS A PURPOSE FOR YOU

We are not here by accident or chance. God had a plan for our lives before we were ever born. And we thought we were a product of our parents. Well, we are; I am a little like my father and a little like my mother. But I am also what God designed me to be. Jeremiah 1:5 New American Standard Version says, "Before I formed you in your mother's womb I knew you." The word "knew" here means "to know by seeing." It's the same word used in Genesis 4:1 for the relationship between husband and wife. God saw you before you were born.

God wanted you and made you for a specific purpose. He wants you to trust him and follow his leading. He wants you to do things according to his plan. I used to work as a production machinist and had to make parts according to the blueprints. If a part was not made according to the blueprint, then the part was not acceptable. I was not allowed to change the blueprint to whatever I thought it should be. God's plan for us is a perfect plan. The problem is that we try to make it better. God knows what he is doing. All we have to do is follow his instructions. It starts by reading the Bible and doing what it says. Also, we must follow the leading of the Holy Spirit, which is that inward feeling that tells us what to do and what not to do.

There seems to be a prevailing thought among many churches today that being poor is spiritual. That cannot be supported with scripture. Third John 2 says, "I wish above all things that thou mayest prosper and be in health, even as thy soul prospereth." Prosperity is more than money but does include money. The word "prosper" includes health and well-being. Deuteronomy 8:18 says, "For it is he that giveth thee power to get wealth." Notice the word "get"—God will not give you money. He will give you the ability. It's up to us to use that ability and to manage our money properly. He wants us to have money. How else will he finance his work? The Bible says the love of money is the root of all evil. There is nothing wrong with money. We must not let money control us. When our children were growing up, we taught them to obey and do what is right because we knew later in life it would help them. We wanted them to trust us and believe us. That is what God wants from us. All God wants of us is to trust him and do what we are told. If we are obedient, the rewards will be tremendous.

GOD CHOSE YOU

But you might say, "I don't feel worthy." Don't worry; you're not. Neither is anyone else. God chose us and made a way for us to be reconciled with him. After Adam's sin there was no way for us to get back to God; he had to make the first move. God created us for a specific purpose. In Jeremiah 1:5, God says, "Before I formed thee in the belly I knew thee; and before thou camest forth out of the womb I sanctified thee, and I ordained thee a prophet unto the nations." God told Jeremiah this when he called him. God also has a purpose for each one of us. He chose us to accomplish that purpose, and if we don't do it, we will miss the blessings of God. No, you were not an accident, even if your parents weren't expecting you. Jeremiah 29:11 (NIV) says, "God knows the plans that he has for you, plans to prosper you and not to harm you, plans to give you a hope and a future." God does not make you sick to teach you a lesson or to get your attention. He does not need to. He got Moses's attention with a burning bush; he talked to Balaam through a donkey; he found Gideon hiding in a wine press; he sent an angel to appear to Zacharias and Mary. He met Saul on the road to Damascus. If God wants your attention, he can get it without hurting you or making you sick.

THERE'S HOPE

God wants us to have hope. That means if we are following God, everything will work out according to God's plan. That does not mean God will put us on the superhighway of life, and we will have no more problems. It does mean God will take us by the hand and walk through it with us. We will still face troubles and trials. It just means God will walk us through them. God wants us to have a future, not just a daily existence. God will show us his plans. It may be one step at a time, but he will lead us through it. God's Word never changes, and his plans do not fail. It's when I try to get him to bless my ideas and plans that there becomes a problem. Romans 4:20–21 says, "He [Abraham] staggered not at the promise of God through unbelief; but was strong in faith, giving glory to God; and being fully persuaded, that what he had promised, he was able also to perform." God can be trusted. What God said he will do, he will do. It may not come to pass when we want it to, but it will when God knows the time is right.

Sometimes it is hard to wait for the promises of God. That's why we need to remember and repeat the promises of God. Repeating the promises of God will keep us in tune with him and make it easier to follow his leading. The Word will give us strength, it will give us hope, and it will help us to build our faith. It should be our road map for life and the very foundation for living. If I were to plan a trip, I would get a road map out or at least use a GPS so I would know how to get to my destination. I would have some kind of direction before I started.

GOD WILL PREVAIL

Isaiah 55:11 says, "So shall my word be that goeth forth out of my mouth: it shall not return unto me void, but it shall accomplish that which I please, and it shall prosper in the thing whereto I sent it." If God said it, it's true. Once God speaks, it is established forever. He will not change his mind. In Matthew 24:35, Jesus says, "Heaven and earth shall pass away, but my words shall not pass away." Romans 11:29 (NASV) says, "The gifts and the callings of God are irrevocable." God wrote the master plan for our lives before we were ever conceived, and he will not change his mind. We cannot beg him, we cannot buy him, and God does not play *Let's Make a Deal.* The plan will never fail, so you might as well give up, give in, and do it God's way. In the end, you will be glad you did. I will fail, I will make mistakes, and I will do things wrong, but God is ever true. When God designed the world and spoke it into being and set Adam and Eve in the Garden of Eden, he had a specific plan in mind for each one of us. If we don't follow that plan, we limit God's ability to work in our lives.

CHOOSING FRIENDS

We should choose our friends wisely—friends that will lift us up and encourage us, not ones that will only take from us and drag us down. Proverbs 17:17 says, "A friend loveth at all times." A friend should step in when the going gets rough, not bail out. They should be there to help and encourage us, not make fun of us and tell us how stupid we were. God wants us to succeed. God will not condemn us or ridicule us.

Not that we should ignore people who need our help. We should always be an encouragement to others and try to lift them up. But we must be careful; if all we do is give out, we will become weak and run down. Your car's battery is continually being charged as you drive. If it doesn't, it will run down, and your car will not work. We need to find people who will encourage us and bring us up to a higher level. We should keep a balance.

SEEK WISDOM FIRST

Seek wisdom first, and the rest will come. Solomon sought wisdom and became the richest man this world has ever seen. But we can also learn from him to keep our eyes on God and not let the wealth gain control of us. First Timothy 6:10 says, "The love of money is the root of all evil," not the money itself. Ecclesiastes 10:19 (NIV) says, "Money is the answer for everything." It takes money to live, but we should not let money control us. Ecclesiastes 5:10 (NIV) says, "Whoever loves money never has enough; whoever loves wealth is never satisfied with his income." The money in itself is not the problem; it's when the money gets control of us. This does not always come easy. It is a learning process. And we never stop learning.

We have to be patient and let God do his work in us and prepare us. If we follow God, even though we may be in the midst of trouble, we can have peace in our hearts because the will of God will not take us to where the grace of God cannot keep us. God will not put us in a place he cannot reach us. He will always be with us. Paul writes in 2 Timothy 2:1, "Be strong in the grace that is in Christ Jesus." The word "strong" means "to empower or enable."

The word "grace" means "unmerited favor" We are able to stand strong because God's graciousness is always willing to forgive and to stand with us in trouble. He is ever present in our lives and wants to keep us in his care. God will not ask us to go somewhere or to do something without being with us each step of the way. He will guide us and lead us through.

Paul was in prison in Rome when he wrote those words and facing certain death at the hands of Nero. A missionary once told me not to pray that God will protect him from persecution but that he will give him staying power. I pondered that statement for several months before it came to me: we all need staying power. We don't know when we will hear words like "cancer" or that a loved one has just passed away. God will not always keep us from troubles, but he will always be with us and will lead us through. That does not mean that the trouble in itself is God's will, but we learn more and remember the lesson better if we have to work through it. God does not hand out sickness and disease.

THERE'S JOY

"The mountains and the hills will break forth before you into singing and all the trees of the field will clap their hands" (Is 55:12). Is that why C. S. Lewis included talking trees in *The Chronicles of Narnia*? God wants you to be happy and joyful. It is a much better witness when you are happy and joyful than when you are sad and gloomy. We need to present something that will attract people to us. Which would be more attractive, someone who is sad and gloomy all the time or someone who is cheerful and happy? I'll take the cheerful and happy person.

All of God's creation will sing his praises. It was Jesus who said if the people don't praise him, the stones would cry out. That's found in Luke 19:40. Even in the midst of trouble, we are to praise God. We can live in peace in the middle of the storm. First Thessalonians 5:18 says, "In everything give thanks: for this is the will of God in Christ Jesus concerning you." Notice the word "in" at the beginning of this verse. God does not say here that we are to praise him for our troubles but in the midst of our troubles. After Paul and Silas had been beaten and cast into the inner prison, they were praying and praising God at midnight, when there was an earthquake, and the gates opened. The story is found in Acts 16:16–31. They asked God for help and then praised him for the answer. We can't ask God for help and then sit in an easy chair and wait for the answer to come.

When our backs are against the wall and there is no place to turn, do we give up or turn to God? When we have done everything we can and can't see the end, we should turn to God and praise him because he promised to see us through. As I said, we should praise him for who he is, regardless of our troubles. In Daniel 3, Shadrach, Meshach, and Abednego refused to bow to the golden image and said in verse 17 and 18, "The God whom we serve is able to save us…but even if he doesn't, we want to make it clear…we will never serve your gods or worship the gold statue you have set up" (NLT). If we can praise God in the midst of our troubles, then regardless of the outcome, we know that God is with us. So when we are facing insurmountable odds, we should praise God anyway.

James 1:5 says, "If any of you lack wisdom let him ask of God that giveth to all men liberally and upbraideth not, and it shall be given him." You have questions; God has answers, and he won't call you dumb or stupid. But once again, we have to read and study the Bible. That's where our answers are found. If we don't understand, God will help us. He will show us. The Holy Spirit will teach us. It may not be what we were expecting or what we wanted to hear, but we can trust God that he will lead us. I have found I learn more by listening than by talking.

CAN YOU HEAR THE SILENCE?

Sometimes we have to learn to listen to the silence. In this twenty-first century, people are afraid of silence. We have iPods, MP3 players, cell phones, and all sorts of things to entertain us. Sometimes we need to shut everything off and sit in quiet reflection and listen to the silence. It allows God to talk to us and help us to understand ourselves. We need to set aside time to be alone with God. You can't rush God. He will take his time. He wants more than five minutes. He wants the first and best of our time, not the leftovers.

Isaiah 40.31 says, "They that wait on upon the Lord shall renew their strength." The word "wait" here has a dual meaning. First, we are to wait on the Lord and for his timing and instruction, and we are to let God lead us and guide us. It's when we get ahead of God and try to do things our way that we get into trouble. I don't like waiting in line or at traffic lights, but they are a part of life. The same is true of God. We need to learn patience and wait on God. But while we are waiting on God, we need secondly to wait on God. Just as a waiter or waitress will come and serve us in a restaurant, we are to do something. It is all a preparation for what God has for us in the future. We have to learn to do the little things before we get to do the big things. Are you a prayer warrior? We all should pray, but for some it is a passion. Can you sing? Can you teach? Can you drive a bus? Do you like to work on cars? Sitting in an easy chair and waiting on God is not a calling. It's an excuse to do nothing.

Winning the Battle

James 4:7 (NASV) says, "Submit therefore to God, resist the devil and he will flee from you." I get a little concerned when people use the second part of that verse without including the first part. If we are to defeat the devil, we have to be close to God. We cannot resist the devil on our own. We need God. When we draw near to God by studying and memorizing his Word, we can use scripture against Satan, and he will not be able to stand against it. We have to make the first move. We have to choose to follow Christ. Once we make the first move, God is right there and will walk with us and be our guide. God will not force himself upon us. God does not carry a big stick and hit us when we don't do what he wants us to. He will give us the choice, but with that choice comes consequences. We need to choose to do the right thing.

Psalm 1:1 says, "Blessed is the man who walketh not in the council of the ungodly, nor standeth in the way of sinners, nor sits in the seat of the scornful." Who are you going to for advice? Who is your council? We all need advice from time to time, but to whom are we going? In Aesop's fable "The Rooster and the Fox," the fox tried to talk the rooster into coming down out of the tree so they could visit. The rooster declined because there were too many animals that wanted him for a meal. The fox claimed that all the animals had agreed to get along. Nobody would hurt him. The rooster noticed a pack of hounds coming their way and told the fox. The fox had to suddenly leave, saying the hounds "might not have heard of the plan yet." The world cannot give us the right kind of advice because the natural mind cannot understand the things of God. God does not use human logic, and people will often not understand the way God does things. To get God's advice, you have to go to God. Proverbs 3:5–6 says, "Trust in the Lord with all thine heart; and lean not unto thine own understanding. In all thy ways acknowledge him, and he shall direct thy paths." We need to give everything to God and let him lead us, and he will take us to places we never thought possible.

What do I mean by giving everything to God? Give him control of your body, soul, and spirit. Colossians 3:2 (NASV) says, "Set your mind on things above, not on things that are on the earth." Galatians 5:16 says, "Walk in the Spirit, and ye shall not fulfill the lust of the flesh." If we put Christ first and seek his guidance, then our spirits will have victory over our flesh. Give him your problems. He will help you through them. Give him your sorrows. He will help you to get over them. Give him your joys. He will multiply them. Joshua 24:15 says, "Choose…whom you will serve." Joshua was challenging the children of Israel to choose which direction they were going to go. Were they going to serve the God that brought them to this land or the gods in whose land they dwelt? We need to do the same thing sometimes. We need to look back and see how far we have come and remember how we got here.

DRAW NEAR

James 4:8 (NASV) says, "Draw near to God and he will draw near to you." You draw near by spending time with him, reading his Word, and praying and waiting on him. If we draw near to him, he will come to us. We cannot serve two masters, and don't try walking the fence—Satan owns the fence. Proverbs 19:20 says, "Hear council and receive instruction." You do that by spending time with God, fellowshipping with other believers, and by being in church on a regular basis. We need to take God with us wherever we go. Whatever we do and wherever we go, we need to always be prepared to ask God for direction. We need to be open to his leading and allow him to guide us in all that we say and do. If we can't take God with us, then maybe we shouldn't go there. Proverbs 3:5 says, "Trust in the Lord with all thine heart; and lean not unto thine own understanding." We need to learn to trust God all the time in all things and stop trying to tell God how to fix our problems. Too many times we go to God with a problem and have it all figured out how he should fix it. That doesn't work. This world is God's design and his making, and he knows exactly how it should be done. We will do it his way, or we will do it without him.

Colossians 3:23 (NASV) says, "Whatever you do, do it heartily as to the Lord." "Heartily" means from our innermost being, from deep down inside. We have to mean it from the heart, not just a bunch of words. We are God's children. Jesus died on the cross for us and rose again to give us victory over Satan. Our walk with Christ needs to be daily and constant. It may seem difficult at first, because it is hard to change our habits, but the more we work at it, the more we will enjoy his company. Galatians 5:16 says, "Walk by the Spirit and ye will not fulfill the lust of the flesh." The word "lust" simply means desiring something we are not supposed to have. If we let the Holy Spirit guide us, we will not get caught up in the things of this world. I understand in today's world we need things like money, cars, houses, and maybe even some toys. We especially like the toys. But we must not let them become our gods. There is nothing wrong with these things as long as we keep God first. As Matthew 6:33 says, "Seek ye first the kingdom of God and his righteousness and all these things shall be added unto you." Don't do what you want and expect God to bless it. One of the keys to receiving God's blessings is obedience. Just as an obedient child is more likely to be in the good graces of his parents, so it is between God and us. If we are obedient, he will do more for us.

Paul says you are in the world but should not be of the world. Romans 12:2 says, "Be not conformed to this world: but be ye transformed by the renewing of your mind." We renew our minds by reading the Word of God, by meditating on the Word of God, and by praying to God.

CHANGE THE FLAVOR

In Matthew 5:13, Jesus says, "Ye are the salt of the earth." In William Barclay's *The Daily Study Bible Series* "The Gospel of Matthew" Barclay gives three special qualities of salt. First, salt was connected with purity. The Christians standards need to be standards of honesty and integrity. We need to be known for our hard work and perseverance. We need to do the right thing even when no one is watching. Second, salt was widely used as a preservative to keep things from going bad. We as Christians need to act as preservatives and have an influence on the lives of those around us. We must hold to the same standards regardless of the influence around us. Third, salt is used as seasoning. It changes the flavor of things. We can change the flavor by holding to the standards God has set before us. That does not mean that everyone will do things the way we say they should be done, but we can still make a difference. Salt also has healing properties. If you have a tooth pulled, the dentist may tell you to gargle with salt water.

NOWHERE TO GO

Stuck in a rut, in a dead end job, with no place to go? God can make a way where there is no way, but obedience is the key. Romans 10:17 says, "Faith cometh by hearing and hearing by the Word of God." Faith is not belief without proof but trust without reservation. Our faith has to be active, acting on what the Word of God tells us to do without knowing the end result or even the next step. Our faith should inspire our actions. James 2:20 says, "Faith without works is dead." If we don't act upon what we say we believe, then it isn't faith. If we say we believe it, then our actions are needed to prove that we believe what we say we believe. No, God does not say we have to understand—just have faith, and believe God. If we understood everything and knew exactly how everything was going to work out, we would not need faith. We worked hard as parents so that our children would trust us. It was our job to teach them right from wrong. As children they did not always understand "whys" and "becauses." We wanted them to trust us and believe we were doing the right thing. That is what God wants us to do—just trust him. God has been around for a long time, and he designed this world. He is omniscient. That means he knows everything. He is capable of handling every situation. We cannot catch God by surprise. Things may not happen as fast as we would like them to when we give our circumstances to God, but rest assured that God will work things out for our good. That does not mean God will put us on a superhighway and everything will be great, but by trusting in him, we will have peace and contentment in our hearts.

STUDY THE CONTRACT

As I said earlier, the Bible is a contract between God and us. God will keep his part, but we have to keep our part to make it work. Obedience is what makes this contract work. Second Chronicles 7:14 says, "If my people who are called by my name, shall humble themselves and pray, and seek my face, and turn from their wicked ways, then will I hear from heaven, and forgive their sin, and will heal their land." Just as in any contract, there are terms to abide by. You have to do your part in order to make the contract work. We have to know what the contract says. The word "contract" is a modern term for the blood covenant in the Old Testament. The definition of "testament" is "covenant, contract, or agreement." The blood covenant was widely practiced throughout the ancient world and was a binding agreement unto death. If a person broke that covenant, his or her own family would seek him out and kill him. Weaker tribes would seek to "cut the covenant," as it was called, with stronger tribes for protection.

Abraham entered into covenant with God. David and Jonathan cut the covenant because of their love for each other. Our celebration of communion is a blood covenant. Each successive family member could enter into that covenant simply by agreeing to the terms without having to go through the rituals again. We must take this contract seriously and understand the terms of the covenant.

That means we have to read and study the Bible for ourselves. We cannot depend on someone else to teach us what it says. We need to read it for ourselves so that we will not be misled.

WE NEED A SHEPHERD

Please don't misunderstand me; we need a pastor. Sheep need a shepherd to keep them from wandering off and getting lost. We need a church to call home. Hebrews 10:24–25 says, "And let us consider one another to provoke unto love and good works: Not forsaking the assembling of ourselves together, as the manner of some is; but exhorting one another: and so much the more, as ye see the day approaching." As much as we need people, God sometimes wants to speak to us directly with no one else around. He wants to get intimate with us. He wants to get personal. It's hard to have intimacy in a roomful of people.

Joshua 1:8 says, "This book of the law shall not depart out of thy mouth; but thou shalt meditate therein day and night, that thou mayest observe to do according to all that is written therein: for then thou shalt make thy way prosperous, and then thou shalt have good success." Second Timothy 2:15 says, "Study to show thyself approved unto God, a workman that needeth not to be ashamed, rightly dividing the word of truth." These two verses tell us to study God's Word. We can have success outside of the Bible, but it will not be good success. If we follow God's Word, we do not need to be ashamed, regardless of what people around us are saying.

In Ezra 7:10 (NASV), Ezra "set in his heart to study the law of the Lord, and to practice it, and to teach his statutes and ordinances in Israel." Ezra had made up his mind to live according to the Word of God. He was going to set the example before the people because that's where teaching starts. We need to live what we say we believe because that's when people will take notice. Daniel 1:8 says, "But Daniel purposed in his heart that he would not defile himself with the portion of the king's meat, nor with the wine which he drank: therefore he requested of the prince of the eunuchs that he might not defile himself." Daniel knew the food that the king was serving them was not allowed by dietary laws set forth in the law because he had read the scriptures. He set forth a plan given to him by God, because God's plans will always work, and he convinced the prince of eunuchs to go along with it. We can be just as victorious as Ezra and Daniel were if we know the Word and appropriate it in our lives. If we study the Word as they did, God can do mighty things through us.

DILIGENCE

In 2 Timothy 2:15, the word "study" means "diligence or persistent effort." It can't be hit and miss or "when I feel like it." Get a Bible dictionary and a concordance and a regular dictionary and study. Ask God to guide you. Allow the Holy Spirit to lead you. You can watch your favorite preacher on television, but don't let that be the only thing that feeds you. We make sure that our physical bodies get fed, but we seem to put our spirits on a starvation diet and then wonder why we can't seem to get ahead or get victory in our battles. We need to feed our spirits by reading, praying, and waiting on God, allowing him to speak to us. First Corinthians 4:5 (NASV) says, "Therefore do not go on passing judgment before the time, but wait until the Lord comes who will both bring to light the things hidden in the darkness and disclose the motives of men's hearts: and then each man's praise will come to him from God." Too often we seek human's approval and leave God out. We should seek God's approval and not worry what people think.

Don't misunderstand this. We can seek advice from humanity, but we need to be careful that people do not draw us away from God. That is why we should study and pray so that human teachings don't draw us away from God. If we don't know the Word of God, then people can mislead us with words that sound good. Don't be afraid to check out what you are told when it doesn't feel right.

FRIENDS

James 2:23 calls Abraham the friend of God. Why? Because he was obedient and faithful, and "it was imputed unto him for righteousness." He not only believed God—he acted on that belief. In Genesis 6:3 (NASV), God said, "My spirit shall not strive with man forever." God and humanity will not always agree. Who are we going to follow? Are we going to follow God, or are we going to follow humanity? God has a much better perspective on everything. Revelation 3:16 says, "Because thou art lukewarm, and neither cold nor hot, I will spue thee out of my mouth." Either you will serve God, or you will serve humanity, but you cannot serve both. We must either choose Christ or choose the world. The word "spue" here means "to vomit." In other words, what Jesus is saying is, "You make me sick." God wants total commitment, not just a Sunday social club. To be an approved workman means to do the will of God, to follow his teachings, and to live by his precepts.

I was told once that doing the will of God is doing the next right thing. Doing the will of God is not always grand and glorious. Many times our work will go unnoticed by nearly everyone. In Matthew 25:34–40 (NASV), Jesus talks about feeding the hungry, giving water to the thirsty, and taking in strangers:

> Then the King will say to those on his right, Come you who
> are blessed of my Father, inherit the kingdom prepared for

you from the foundation of the world. For I was hungry, and you gave me something to eat; I was thirsty and you gave me drink; I was a stranger, and you invited me in; naked and you clothed me; I was sick, and you visited me; I was in prison and you came to Me. Then the righteous will answer Him, saying, Lord, when did we see You hungry, and feed You, or thirsty and give You drink? And when did we see You a stranger, and invite You in, or naked and clothe You? And when did we see You sick, or in prison, and come to You? And the King will answer and say to them, Truly I say to you, to the extent that you did it to one of these brothers of mine, even the least of them, you did it to Me.

We need to learn to do the little things and keep a smile on our faces. We need to help those around us, be a friend to those we work with, and encourage those we see every day.

CHRIST IN ME

Our lives and lifestyle should be such that they will present Christ. People should look at us, see that we are different, and want to know why. We should be kinder, more helpful, and easier to get along with. Our lives should always be witnesses, and we should be ready to talk if we have to. Proverbs 3:27 says, "Withhold not good from them to whom it is due when it is in the power of thine hand to do it." We need to help people along the way just because they need help, not to be noticed or to gain a reward. God will not ask you to do something that you are not capable of doing. So if God has asked you to do something, you will be able to accomplish it even if it seems impossible, because God will not ask you to do something you are not capable of doing. And I believe doing the will of God may very well involve a miracle.

Many times we miss out because we are looking for the grand and glorious and don't do the little things. We need to start with the little things and develop them into big things. God gives simple plans that need to be developed. God expects us to work. He wants us to work for him. He will not dump a high-paying job in our laps or give us that mansion on the hill. Deuteronomy 8:18 says, "But thou shalt remember the Lord thy God: for it is he that giveth thee power to get wealth." God has given us the ability to make money, but it is up to us to do it. He will not do it for us, but we do need to listen to him for instructions. Revelation 2:2 says that God knows your works. When God sees things being done because they need to be done and not because you want to be noticed, he will reward you openly. You have to grow into the job. To be an Olympic gold medalist takes years of hard work. It doesn't just happen.

NO SHAME

Romans 1:16 says, "I am not ashamed of the gospel of Christ." We will be different. We will go against the grain. We need to stand on God's Word, and that will not often be popular. We must know the Word of God if we are to have victory over sickness, disease, finances, and the devil. Jesus says in Matthew 10:33, "But whosoever shall deny me before men, him will I also deny before my Father which is in heaven." Sometimes we deny him by keeping silent. Do people know where we stand? Do they know we are Christians? Can they tell there is something different about us? Jesus is our advocate. Hebrews 4:15 says, "For we have not an high priest which cannot be touched with the feeling of our infirmities; but was in all points tempted like as we are, yet without sin." Hebrews 7:25 says, "He [Jesus] ever liveth to make intercession for them." But continued disobedience will break the relationship between God and us, because if we don't follow God and his precepts, he cannot help us. It is up to us to keep that relationship with Christ going. We also need to watch our words because they are powerful. They are much more powerful than we realize. Matthew 12:36–37 says, "Every idle word that men shall speak, they shall give account thereof in the day of judgment. For by thy words thou shalt be justified, and by thy words thou shalt be condemned." The word "idle" here means unproductive. Matthew 18:18 says, "Whatsoever ye shall bind on earth shall be bound in heaven: and whatsoever you shall loose on earth shall be loosed in heaven." Our words will either release God's power or bind it up.

First Peter 3:15 says, "But sanctify the Lord God in your hearts: and be ready always to give an answer to every man that asketh you a reason of the hope that is in you." Why do we believe what we believe? Why did Jesus come? What is salvation? What will salvation do for me? What is the leading of the Holy Spirit? What is the baptism of the Holy Spirit? How do I make all this work for me? Many times we don't talk about Christ because we lack confidence, and we lack confidence because we don't know what the Word says. We get so busy with life that we tend to push God aside. Our relationship with Christ is what needs to be first and remain constant.

In the parable of the fig tree in Matthew 24:32–44, Jesus says we will know the season of his coming. We know that Jesus will return for his church, and the signs of the times are all around us. Verse 37 says that it will be "as in the days of Noah." The people were living for self and self-gratification, and suddenly it was too late. The end is near, and we must be prepared because we don't know exactly when he will return. Let us do as Matthew 5:16 says and "let our light so shine before men that they may see our good works and glorify our Father which is in heaven."

We must live for Christ and put him first, not try to do things our way and of our choosing.

In Ezra 7:10 (NASV), "Ezra set in his heart to study the law of the Lord, and to practice it, and to teach His statutes and ordinances in Israel." Ezra made a plan. He was going to study, use what he learned, and teach it to others. First he was going to study. Psalm 119:11 says, "Thy word have I hid in my heart that I might not sin against thee." We have to read the instruction manual if we are to do things correctly. Psalm 119:105 says, "Thy word is a lamp unto my feet and a light unto my path." His Word will light the way for us. If we were to make a trip across the country, we would make sure we knew how to get there. Too many times we wander through life wondering why we don't get ahead. Matthew 6:33 says, "Seek ye first the Kingdom of God, and his righteousness; and all these things shall be added unto you." God has far more in store for us than we are tapping into because we don't know what his Word says, and we don't follow his leading.

SEEK KNOWLEDGE

Hosea 4:6 says, "Because we have rejected knowledge he will reject us." God will not force us to study or pray. We have to do it on our own. You can run from God for a long time, and as soon as you stop, he is right there. It is a choice. We have to choose to follow God. We have to choose to read and apply his Word, but we will never walk alone. We can find many stories from the Bible of how people used the Word to get victory. That's why we need to read it. If we are to walk the path that God wants us to walk, we have to know the truth of his Word. As I said, it is important to have a church home and attend. It is important to have a pastor because you need that covering. We need leadership; we need guidance; we need someone to keep us going in the right direction. The pastor is the head of the church as the husband is the head of the family. Though God wants to talk to us directly, sometimes we also need to hear from the pastor. He is appointed by God to lead us. In the Old Testament, the prophets and priests had the responsibility of maintaining the purity of God's Word. Today the pastor has that responsibility. That is what he has been called to do. His job is to teach and preach to the people God has given him and to lead them in the right direction. But it is equally important for each of us to have an intimate relationship with Jesus Christ.

The Bible was written by humans but directed by the Holy Spirit. Each writer used his own style, but he wrote what God inspired him to write. This means that God used people as the tool to write; humans wrote in terms that we understood. As a friend of mine told me, when God says something once, you should take note; if he says it twice, you had better listen; and if he says it three times, you had better pay attention. Whatever God speaks stands throughout eternity. Matthew 24:35 says, "Heaven and earth shall pass away, but my words shall not pass away. It will never change. Second Peter 1:21 says, "Prophecy came not by the will of man, but holy men of God spake as they were moved by the Holy Ghost." Humans did not dream the Bible up. They were just doing what they were told. We did not evolve from anything. Please don't downgrade the monkeys. The universe and all that is in it was designed and built by God. Second Timothy 3:16–17 says, "All scripture is given by inspiration of God and is profitable for doctrine, for reproof, for correction, for instruction in righteousness, that the man of God may be perfect thoroughly furnished unto all good works." The word "all" here means "everything included." The Bible is the written Word of God and was given to us divinely breathed, or God breathed. Everything from Genesis to Revelation is God's Word, instructions for us to follow in order to live for him. It is profitable for us to live by those instructions. If we are going to receive the blessings of God, we must follow his leading.

INSTRUCTIONS

Don't let the word "doctrine" scare you. It simply means "instruction." It's just the basis on which we build. For example, the Ten Commandments were the basis for the law in the Old Testament. Every church has "tenets of faith" or articles of faith. That is their doctrine or basic beliefs that they use as a foundation to build on. "Reproof" means "to admonish or convict." The Bible teaches us what God expects; it tells us how to act and live. It corrects us when we are wrong. It keeps us going in the right direction. "Correction" means "a straightening up again and again and again." We must never give up; we can be reformed with God's help. Luke 1:37 says, "With God nothing shall be impossible." God wants us to be happy, healthy, and blessed, but we must let the Holy Spirit instruct us, educate us, and train us in the paths of righteousness. We need to allow God through the Holy Spirit to teach us and show us how to live. I am not trying to say God will put us on a superhighway and that we will not face problems or troubles. That is not the case, but he will walk with us and take us by the hand and lead us through. We just need to trust him because he is faithful to those who follow his Word.

FAITH

"Faith" means "firm persuasion; a conviction based upon hearing." Hebrews 11:1 says, "Faith is the substance of things hoped for, the evidence of things not seen." Abraham's faith was not in God's promises. That was the occasion of its exercise. His faith rested in God himself. In the gospels, people followed Jesus because of the miracles he performed, not because he was God. When the trials came, everyone scattered, including the disciples. Our faith needs to be in God himself. This really has to do with the character of God. Is God who he says he is? Does God keep his Word? Can I really trust God? These are the questions we have to answer for ourselves. If I put my faith and trust in God, will he let me down? Hebrews 11:6 says, "Without faith it is impossible to please God." We need to believe in God, who he is, what he is, and that he will remain true to his Word. By doing this, we are exercising our faith and putting it to work for us. James 2:17 says, "Even so faith, if it hath not works is dead." In order for it to be faith, it requires action.

In Hebrews 11:1, the word "substance" means "a setting under, support, the foundation." In order for things to stand the test of time, they must have a firm foundation. The wise man built his house upon the rock because he knew that storms would come. Matthew 7:24–25 says, "Therefore whosoever heareth these sayings of mine, and doeth them, I will liken him unto a wise man, which built his house upon a rock: And the rains descended, and the floods came, and the winds blew, and beat upon that house; and it fell not: for it was founded upon a rock." To build a building, you first dig down before you build up. You need to go deep enough to establish a solid foundation, a foundation that will stand up against the test of time. Marriages don't last today because there was never a firm foundation in the beginning. Romans 10:17 says, "Faith cometh by hearing and hearing by the Word of God." We must build a firm foundation on the Word of God for our faith to carry us through. Doing the will of God will require a miracle. That's what faith is all about: believing that God will take us beyond our human abilities. Then we will know that it was not us but God who caused all this to happen. Faith is needed to receive the miracles. To get a conviction in a court of law, you need evidence; you need proof. For faith to work, you need proof, and reading God's Word gives you the proof you need. Numbers 23:19 says, "God is not a man that he should lie." If God said it, he will do it.

START SMALL

Matthew 17:20 and Mark 4:31 both talk about faith as a grain of mustard seed. There are three things about the mustard seed mentioned here that we should look at.

1. The mustard seed is one of the smallest of seeds. Romans 12:3 says, "God hath dealt to every man the measure of faith." It is up to us to develop that measure of faith. Just as we would plant the mustard seed, we need to plant that "measure of faith" in our hearts and feed it God's Word. God doesn't give great ideas; he gives simple ideas that we need to develop. We have to start small, be faithful in the

little things, and let God lead us to bigger things. God will not give us the big things until we prove we can do the little things faithfully. Too many times we want to go straight to the big things without learning the things that we need to know when we get to the top. You don't start out as a CEO of a major corporation. You have to work your way up.

2. The mustard seed is an annual. That means you have to plant it every year. It does not come up by itself. That's the way it is with our faith. We must keep planting it on a regular basis. We plant it by reading the Bible and seeing what God has done in the past. Knowing that God never changes, we know that he will do the same for us too. It will establish a pattern that we can follow because we know that "God will never leave us nor forsake us" (Heb 13:5). By reading God's Word, we can see that others walked by faith; and if it worked for them, we know it will work for us too. God asked Abraham, "Is anything too hard for God?" (Gn 18:14). Faith will not rise up within us unless we feed it the Word of God.

3. The mustard seed, when cultivated and cared for in good fertile soil, will grow ten to twelve feet tall in a single season. Reading and studying the Word of God will cultivate our hearts so faith will grow. We need the right nutrients so faith can grow. Staying in touch with God by maintaining a relationship with him will give us those nutrients.

ARMED WITH THE WORD

Hebrews 4:12 says, "For the Word of God is quick, and powerful, and sharper than a two edged sword, piercing even to the dividing asunder of soul and spirit, and of the joints and marrow, and is a discerner of the thoughts and intents of the heart." "Word" here is the Greek word "logos," or the written Word of God. God gave the writers of the Bible what to say, and they wrote it down. God gave them the thought, and they wrote it in terms that they understood. Second Peter 1:20–21 says, "Knowing this first, that no prophecy of the scripture is of any private interpretation. For the prophecy came not in old time by the will of man: but holy men of God spake as they were moved by the Holy Ghost." It is the foundation of God's plan for his people. Everything that God does today will be in line with the written Word of God. God, which is "Theos" in the Greek, translates (with few exceptions) in Hebrew to the words "Elohim" and "Jehovah," the former expressing his fullness of divine power and the latter declaring his divine self-existence.

"Quick" here means "to live, be alive." I believe it carries with it the thought of more than just existing or breathing. It means really being alive, feeling alive, enjoying life, and being happy and excited—that's what God can do for us. God never intended for us to live boring, mundane lives. Our lives should be such that others want to know why we are different. Proverbs 29:18 says, "Where there is no vision, the people perish, but happy is he that keepeth the law." Psalm 37:23 says, "A good man's steps are ordered of the Lord and he delighteth in his way." To find true happiness and joy, we need to follow God's plan for our lives. Ann Landers once said, "Happiness is a by-product." If we pursue happiness, we will never be satisfied; if we pursue God, happiness will come.

"Powerful" means "active and able." The Word is able to do what it says and is active in doing it, but it is up to us to make it alive and active in our lives. "Sharper" means "to cut as if by a single stroke." When going into battle, a soldier fells each enemy as quickly as possible. When doing battle with the enemy, Satan, you will need the Word of God to win that battle.

"Two-edged" means "double edged." A double-edged sword is more effective in battle. "Piercing" means "to reach through or penetrate." The Word of God will penetrate into our hearts and divide or separate what is from our own minds and what is from God. It will discern what are our thoughts and intentions. The Word of God will teach us and correct us. Second Timothy 3:16 says, "All scripture is given by inspiration of God, and is profitable for doctrine, for reproof, for correction, for instruction in righteousness." We need to know what the Word of God says. It is our guide, our road map for life.

We also need to "not forsake the assembling of ourselves together" (Heb 10:25). This is a team effort. We need to work together. God did not design us to work alone. We need the encouragement of others, and we need to encourage them. We need people.

God has given us the measure of faith. Romans 12:3 says, "For I say, through the grace given unto me, to every man that is among you, not to think of himself more highly than he ought to think; but to think soberly, according as God hath dealt to every man the measure of faith." It is up to us to exercise that faith and make it strong. I do not believe God give us big ideas. He gives simple ideas that with his help we can develop. It takes faith to see a miracle. It takes believing that God knows what he is doing—because we can't see it—to make things happen. It takes faith to know God will be with us and guide us through. Hebrews 13:5 says, "God will never leave us or forsake us." By reading God's Word and seeing what he has done for others, we know that God will always be as close as the mention of his name.

"What can faith do for me?" you might ask. For Abraham, faith provided a sacrifice so that he did not have to sacrifice his son Isaac. By faith Noah built a boat because God said it was going to rain, though it had never rained. Through faith Sarah had a baby at the age of ninety. Through faith Joseph went from jailbird to prime minister. Through faith Moses chose affliction with his own people rather than sin for a season. By faith Rahab was spared from destruction. By faith Gideon defeated a combined army of 120,000 soldiers with three hundred men.

WE HAVE WITNESSES

Hebrews 12:1–2 says, "Wherefore seeing we are compassed about with so great a cloud of witnesses, let us lay aside every weight, and the sin which doth so easily beset us, and let us run with patience the race that is set before us, Looking unto Jesus the author and finisher of our faith; who for the joy that was set before him endured the cross, despising the shame, and is set down at the right hand of the throne of God." This is why we have the Bible—to learn about God and what God has done in the past and what he plans to do in the future. We build our faith by reading what God has done in the past, and we know he will do it for us too. Sometimes we need to quit trying to make it happen and let God do what he said he would do. By faith, we have to get out of his way. It is easy to get caught up in working to provide for our families and let work become a trap—not that we shouldn't work, since God uses that to provide for us. But our family comes first, and if we have faith, God will guide us and teach us and lead us to where he wants us. Maybe it's more education, a different job, a promotion, or starting our own business. We have to let God show us the way. We have to look to Jesus; he is the one who authored faith, and he has experienced life "He was in all points tempted like as we are" (Heb 4:15). The Word of God is full of promises. It is up to us to know them and claim them.

PRAYER

*U*nger's *Bible Dictionary* defines prayer as "an expression of dependence upon God," so one must ask the question, "Based upon my prayer life, how much am I really depending upon God?" Too many times our prayer lives are lacking, which brings me to another point. John Wesley said, "It seems God is limited by our prayer life, that he can do nothing for humanity unless we ask Him." In Gordon Lindsay's book *Prayer That Moves Mountains*, he recounts this story: A Christian Armenian merchant was transporting merchandise by caravan across the desert to a town in Turkish Armenia. He was raised in a Christian home and daily committed himself to the hands of God. At the time, the country was infested with bandits who robbed caravans. Unknown to the merchant, these bandits had been following his caravan, intending to rob it at the first camping place on the plains.

After dark, at the designated time, the bandits drew close to the camp. Everything was strangely quiet (no guards or watchmen). But as they came nearer, to their astonishment, they saw high walls standing around the caravan.

They tried again the next night and found the same impassable walls. On the third night, the walls were standing, but there were broken places through which the bandits could enter.

Terrified by the mystery, the captain of the bandits awakened the merchant. "What does this mean? Ever since you left Ezerum, we followed you, intending to rob you. The first and second night, we found high walls around the caravan, but tonight, we entered broken places. If you will tell us the secret behind this, we will not harm you."

The merchant himself was surprised and puzzled. "My friends," he said, "I have done nothing to raise walls around us. All I do is pray every evening, committing myself and those with me to God. I fully trust in him to keep me from evil. But tonight, because I was very tired and sleepy, I made a rather half-hearted prayer. That must be why you were allowed to break through!"

The bandits were overwhelmed by this testimony. Immediately, they gave their lives to Jesus Christ and were saved. From caravan robbers, they became God-fearing men. And the Armenian merchant never forgot the breach in the wall of prayer.

There are different kinds of prayer, and we must follow the rules of each different kind. Just as there are rules for different sports, there are rules for different kinds of prayer. You don't use basketball rules for football, and you don't use hockey rules for baseball. We need to know which rules are for which prayer.

The Bible does not tell us to pray to Jesus. We pray to the Father in Jesus's name. In John 16:23 Jesus says, "Whatsoever ye shall ask the Father in my name, he will give it you." In Hebrews 4:1–5 it says that Jesus is our high priest. Just as the Israelites in the Old Testament went to the high priest, we have to pray to the Father in Jesus's name. Let's look at some different kinds of prayer.

THE PRAYER OF FAITH

Mark 11:23–24 says, "For verily I say unto you, that whosoever shall say unto this mountain, be thou removed, and be thou cast into the sea; and shall not doubt in his heart, but shall believe that those things which he saith shall come to pass; he shall have whatsoever he saith. Therefore I say unto you, what things so ever ye desire, when you pray, believe that ye receive them, and ye shall have them."

The prayer of faith is always based on God's revealed will. God's revealed will never contains the word "if." When the Bible says, "By his stripes we were healed" (2 Pt 2:24), that means disease and pain are gone. When God says he will protect us, he will protect us. Without faith there is no point in praying, because prayer takes faith, and sometimes it takes a lot of faith. William Barclay, in his commentary on the gospel of Mark in the *Daily Study Bible Series,* gives three rules for prayer.

1. It must be a prayer of faith. The phrase about moving mountains was quite common. The phrase was regularly used in reference to removing difficulties. If you didn't understand something and someone explained it to you, they had removed a mountain. So the phrase means that if we have real faith, prayer is a power that can solve any problem and help us deal with difficulty. But to receive the answer, we have to do two things. First, we have to be willing to take our problems to God and leave them there. We have to let God tell us how he is going to solve the problem and not try to tell God how to solve it. We must be sure that what we are asking is in line with God's Word and that we are not trying to justify something we want and are not supposed to have. Second, we need to accept God's guidance when he gives us the answer. It is common to ask for advice when all we really want is approval for our desires.

2. It must be a prayer of expectation. I believe that anything tried in a spirit of confident expectation has a much greater chance of success. The patient who goes to the doctor with no confidence in the prescribed remedies has far less chance of recovery than the patient who is confident that the doctor can cure him or her. Prayer cannot and must not become a formality. It must never be a ritual of hope.

3. It must be a prayer of love. The prayer of a bitter person cannot penetrate the wall of his or her own bitterness. Why? If we are to speak with God, there must be some bond between us. We must have something in common. If the ruling principle of our hearts is bitterness, and God is love, there is a barrier there that will prohibit the prayers being answered. The prayer must be out of love.

The prayer of Consecration

In Luke 22:42, Jesus prays, "Father, if thou be willing, remove this cup from me; nevertheless not my will, but thine, be done." This is a prayer of consecration saying, "I will do whatever you ask of me and whatever you have called me to do. I will not dwell on what I might face in the physical but will focus on what you have called me to do, knowing that your grace is sufficient to keep me." Jesus prayed this prayer in the Garden of Gethsemane the night of his betrayal. He was very honest with his Father and said, "I would rather not go through this; nevertheless, I will do what you have called me to do." It is OK for us to be honest with God and tell him what's on our minds, but we need to commit our lives to Christ and do what he has asked of us. If we give our problems to God and let him make something good out of them, we will be stronger—maybe not in our own strength, but knowing God can handle everything it will make us stronger. Our strength is in the Lord, not in ourselves. The easy path leads to nowhere. We never learn perseverance if we don't face any obstacles. It's how we face those obstacles that makes the difference. We need to take those problems to God.

THE PRAYER OF COMMITMENT

1 Peter 5:7 says, "Casting all your care upon him; for he careth for you." The Amplified Bible says it this way: "Casting the whole of your care—all your anxieties, all your worries, all your concerns, once and for all—on him; for He cares for you affectionately, and cares about you watchfully." When you commit your cares to God, you must leave them there. Don't go to God and give him all your troubles, and when you leave his presence, pick them up again. Psalm 37:5 says, "Commit thy way unto the Lord: trust also in him; and he shall bring it to pass." The word "you" is understood in these statements: *you* cast your cares; *you* commit your way; *you* trust in him. You have to do it before God can bring it to pass. It may not happen immediately, but don't give up. Your faith must carry you through. Matthew 11:28 says, "I [Jesus] will give you rest." If we learn of Jesus, we will learn that he will take care of us, and we need not worry. We need to learn to tell our problems how big our God is, not tell our God how big our problems are. Too often we spend all our time talking about our problems and don't get around to finding answers. If we spend our time encouraging our children and telling them they can succeed, they are more likely to do just that than if we tell them they are no good and will never amount to anything. The same is true for us. We need to be positive and talk solutions and not spend all our time on the problem.

PRAYER OF WORSHIP

Luke 24:52–53 says, "They worshipped him...and were continually in the temple, praising and blessing God." Prayer, praise, and worship are intertwined in that they all three are ways that we stay in touch with God. Praise is singing adoration to God and thanking him for his many blessings. We need to do this regardless of how we feel. First Thessalonians 5:18 says, "In everything give thanks." It does not say *for* everything give thanks. It does not matter what our situation is. We must lift our hands and praise God.

As I said, praise and worship are closely related but yet different. Worship, I believe, takes us past the singing and praising, and we may in silence or with a great noise bask in the presence of God. We need to make time to be silent before God and allow him to work in us. This may not be exactly the same for each person, but we need to allow God to lead us to where he wants us. We may not see the complete picture, but we know by faith that he will not take us to where he cannot protect us. We need to make time for him. Many of us are competitive by nature, and some allow the cares of this world to take control. Sometimes we need to stop and listen to God. Dr. Archibald Hart, in his book *Thrilled to Death,* says that Americans are the most impatient people on earth. We don't like waiting in line at the supermarket or waiting at stoplights, and we don't like being put on hold when we are on the phone. If we can't wait patiently for these things, we will find it hard to "wait on God."

PRAYER OF AGREEMENT

Matthew 18:18–20 says, "Verily I say unto you, whatsoever ye shall bind on earth shall be bound in heaven: and whatsoever you shall loose on earth shall be loosed in heaven. Again I say unto you, that if two of you shall agree on earth as touching anything that they shall ask, it shall be done for them of my Father, which is in heaven. For where two or three are gathered in my name, there am I in the midst of them." The prayer of agreement is asking one, two, or a group to agree with you for a specific need. It is simply calling someone up and asking him or her to agree with you in prayer for something. This is where we need to find people who agree with us doctrinally. We don't want someone praying for us who says, "If it be God's will, we will be healed." We know the Bible says "we are healed"Isa 53:5. and we need to be in agreement about what the scripture says.

PRAYER IN THE SPIRIT

First Corinthians 14:14–15 says, "For if I pray in an unknown tongue, my spirit prayeth, but my understanding is unfruitful. What is it then? I will pray with the spirit, and I will pray with the understanding also: I will sing with the spirit, and I will sing with the understanding also." Praying in the Spirit is praying in an unlearned tongue. It is praying in a language given by the Holy Spirit that we have not learned. Sometimes when we pray, we don't know what to pray. By praying in the Spirit, we are able to pray as God would have us to pray. It is allowing the Holy Spirit to pray through us. To receive the "baptism with the Holy Spirit" is much the same as receiving salvation. Ask, and you shall receive, whether you are by yourself or in a group seeking the same thing. You let the Holy Spirit fill you, and you will begin to speak in a language you did not learn. Your brain will not understand it because you are not using your brain. You are allowing the Holy Spirit to pray through you.

UNITED PRAYER

In Acts 4:24, it says, "They lifted up their voices to God with one accord." United prayer is a gathering together to pray for a united goal. The pastor may call a prayer meeting for a specific need or a weekly prayer meeting to pray for the church and its continuing needs. Though it is important to have a personal prayer time with God, it is also important to band together at times for a specific need. We don't have to wait for the pastor to call the prayer meeting. We can call some people together for a special need. This can be a one-time prayer meeting, or it can be a regular prayer meeting.

PRAYER OF SUPPLICATION

Philippians 4:6 says, "Be careful for nothing: but in everything by prayer and supplication with thanksgiving let your requests be made known to God." Supplication is more than a simple asking. It is a humble entreaty or request. It is not a "pray one time, and you're done." It is staying with it until the answer comes. Daniel prayed for three weeks before he got the answer (see Dn 10). Daniel did not set out to pray for three weeks for the answer. He set out to pray until he got the answer, and it took three weeks for the answer to come. There are some times that spiritual forces have to do battle with the enemy before they can bring us the answer. They need our prayers to defeat that enemy. We live in an instant society and want everything right away. It does not work that way with God. Sometimes we need to persevere until the answer comes.

INTERCESSORY PRAYER

Ezekiel 22:30–31 (NASV) says, "I searched for a man among them who should build up the wall and stand in the gap before Me for the land, that I should not destroy it, but found no one. Thus I poured out my indignation on them; I have consumed them with the fire of my wrath; their way I have brought upon their heads, declares the Lord God." In the preceding verses in chapter 22, Ezekiel gave a list of the sins that Israel had committed. In verse 30, God was looking for someone to stand in the gap and intercede for them but could not find anyone, so he had to punish them. Intercessory prayer is standing in the gap for a person or people who have brought judgment on themselves. Abraham stood in the gap for Lot (see Gn 18:16–33). Jesus stood in the gap for Peter. In Luke 22:31–32, Jesus told Peter, "Satan hath desired to have you, that he may sift you as wheat: But I have prayed for thee, that thy faith fail not." Do we have family members, loved ones, or friends who are not saved or living for the Lord? God needs us to pray for them so that he may work in their hearts. God is not able to work on this earth except through us and our prayers because he has no legal right to govern this world. He lost that legal right when Satan swindled it from Adam. He needs us so that he can work through us to accomplish his plans for this world.

DISCIPLINE

Merriam-Webster's Dictionary defines "discipline" as follows:

"1. Training that corrects, molds, or perfects the mental faculties or moral character.
2a. Control gained by enforcing obedience or order. b. Orderly or prescribed conduct or pattern of behavior.
3. A rule or system of rules governing conduct or activity."

Discipline is what gets us up to go to work every day. It's what keeps us in shape physically, mentally, and spiritually. It can make the difference between a good athlete and a great athlete. It helps us to control our weight or our tongues or our attitudes. Discipline is why we succeed or fail. It will make us or break us. We all seem to have discipline in some areas and not others. We may be able to control our eating habits but have trouble making it to work on time. I am a firm believer in the saying that if you want things to change, you have to change things. You have to make the changes necessary to accomplish the desired result. God will not do it for you. He created you with a free will and will not force you to do anything. The choices you have may seem to force you to make changes, but God will not force you to make those changes. The choice is yours. Your choices in life determine your future. Where do you want to go, and what do you want to accomplish? Make sure those choices help you to get there. Many a career has been slowed or sidelined because of poor choices. Set a goal, and make choices that help you reach that goal.

POOR DISCIPLINE

In Exodus 32, Aaron did not use discipline. The crowd got out of control and had Aaron make a golden calf. Three thousand people lost their lives. Sometimes our lack of discipline can be costly to others or to us. Ignorance of the law is no excuse; neither is ignorance of the Bible. Just a few minutes a day with God can make a big difference. In Colossians 2:5 (NASV), Paul said that he was "rejoicing to see your good discipline and the stability of your faith." If you exercise some discipline and learn the Word of God, you will be prepared when tests and trials come. You will have built up your faith in order to stand on the Word of God. You will know that God is there and that he cares enough to take you by the hand and lead you through. Hebrews 13:5 says, "I will never leave thee, nor forsake thee." Yes, we will face troubles and trials. We can't stop them from coming, but we can be prepared for them and be ready to stop them before they get a foothold in our lives. When we speak the Word of God, we stop Satan in his tracks, and he has no power against us. We know the trials will come, so let's build a firm foundation that the storms cannot break down.

Proverbs 3:11–12 says, "My son, despise not the chastening of the Lord; neither be weary of his correction. For whom the Lord loveth he correcteth; even as a father the son in whom he delight-eth." Proverbs 10:17 says, "He is in the way of life that keepeth instruction: but he that refuseth reproof [discipline] erreth." I remember discipline when I was a child. It usually involved a belt.

The least I learned was I had done something wrong and not to do it again. When I grew up and had children of my own, all those lessons began to make much more sense to me. Suddenly all those lessons became much more real. It was amazing how smart my parents became in such a short time. But then Proverbs 12:1 says, "Whoso loveth instruction loveth knowledge: but he that hateth reproof is brutish." Proverbs 13:1 says, "A wise son heareth his father's instruction." Godly discipline is not always fun, but it is profitable, and the wise will learn from it. Just as an earthly father will correct his children, so will our heavenly Father correct us. Proverbs 29:17 says, "Correct thy son, and he shall give thee rest; yea, he shall give delight unto thy soul."

Just as an Olympic athlete disciplines himself and receives the reward at the end, so must we discipline ourselves, knowing that God has many blessings in store for us if we obey him. First Corinthians 9:24–27 says, "Know ye not that they which run in a race run all, but one receiveth the prize? So run that ye may obtain. And every man that striveth for the mastery is temperate in all things. Now they do it to obtain a corruptible crown; but we have an incorruptible. I therefore so run, not as uncertainly; so fight I, not as one that beateth the air: But I keep under my body, and bring it into subjection: lest that by any means, when I have preached to others, I myself should be a castaway." Discipline brings victory. It takes tremendous discipline to stay with our regimen when no one is watching, but when the test comes and we make it through, then it is clear that we disciplined ourselves and that we stayed with the program. Second Timothy 2:5 says, "And if a man also strive for masteries, yet he is not crowned, except he strive lawfully." We must follow the rules. I think part of our problem is that we are trying to understand the Bible with a democratic mind-set. The Bible is not a democracy. It is a theocracy, which means that God rules. You don't get a vote. You do it God's way, or it doesn't happen. Joshua 24:15 says, "Choose you this day whom you will serve." It is your choice: you can go the way of the world, or you can choose to follow God. He created you with a free will, and he will not beat you over the head with a big stick if you choose the world. But make no mistake. You will reap what you sow, whether it be good or bad.

MAKE A PLAN

As I've said, I am a firm believer in the adage "If you want things to change, you have to change things," but that is easier said than done. You have to make the necessary changes to accomplish the desired result. Habakkuk 2:2 says, "Write the vision and make it plain." Proverbs 29:18 says, "Where there is no vision, the people perish: but he that keepeth the law, happy is he." Psalm 37:23 says, "The steps of a good man are ordered of the Lord: and he delighteth in his way." We need to make plans. Write out your goals, clearly defining each step that is needed to reach that goal and setting aside time each day to spend with God. The commander doesn't lead his troops into battle without a plan and knowing full well what the enemy's capabilities are. The commander may even look for an alliance with another army to strengthen the army's position. Without God we cannot defeat Satan. We need to keep God on our side. He is the alliance we need to defeat Satan. Romans 8:31 says, "If God be for us, who can stand against us?"

If you don't have a daily devotion time with God, don't start out with an hour. That is too big a step. Start with ten or fifteen minutes, and let it grow from there. Pick whatever time of day suits you best. God will be available. You may want to take extra time once in a while to study verses that you have always wondered about. As for study materials, get a *Strong's Concordance* and a Bible dictionary and a regular dictionary. Commentaries are OK, but remember that they are just someone's opinion. They are good for explaining the time period in which the scripture was written, which does help to understand the verse you are studying. You can also use a topical concordance, which gives a list of verses on a specific topic. Don't rush it. Take your time, and allow God to speak to you. It may not be an audible voice, but he will let you know what the scriptures mean if you allow him to. Always be open to the Lord's leading. You will see things you have never seen before, and that may shake your theology. That means you might have to give up some religious teaching. Always look for other verses to support what you find; don't build a doctrine on just one verse. Joshua 1:8 says, "This book of the law shall not depart out of thy mouth; but thou shalt meditate therein day and night, that thou mayest observe to do according to all that is written therein: for then thou shalt make thy way prosperous, and then thou shalt have good success." Second Timothy 2:15 says, "Study to show thyself approved unto God, a workman that needeth not to be ashamed, rightly dividing the word of truth." Both of these verses tell us if we follow God's Word, we will be successful.

We must also spend time in prayer for our families, our pastors, our churches, and missionaries. Paul writes in 1 Timothy 2:1–2, "I exhort therefore, that, first of all, supplications, prayers, intercessions, and giving of thanks, be made for all men; for kings, and for all that are in authority." We need to pray for all who are in leadership over us, pastors, teachers, and all government officials. In 1 Corinthians 1:4, Paul writes, "I thank my God always on your behalf, for the grace of God which is given you by Jesus Christ." In Philippians 1:3–4, he writes, "I thank my God upon every remembrance of you, always in every prayer of mine for you all making request with joy." In Colossians 1:3, he writes, "We give thanks to God and the Father of our Lord Jesus Christ, praying always for you." In 1 Thessalonians 1:2, he writes, "We give thanks to God always for you all, making mention of you in our prayers." Paul prayed for the people he had ministered to, which included his children in the Lord. If your church has a good missions program, you may want to pick one or two missionaries that God lays on your heart rather than trying to pray for all of them. Once again, start small, and build up to where you want to be. Don't try to make giant steps. It can be too discouraging. We need to allow time for God to speak to us. We can't sit down and tell God we have five minutes and expect God to respond.

DON'T RUSH GOD

You don't rush God. We sometimes get in a big hurry and don't take the time we need for what's really important. Matthew 6:33 says, "Seek ye first the Kingdom of God, and his righteousness; and all these things shall be added unto you." If we seek God first and put him first in our lives, then we don't need to get stressed out and try to figure it out ourselves. If we will give it to God and do it his way, it will be easier. I know walking by faith will stretch us sometimes, but if we keep repeating God's Word, we will make it through. By repeating God's Word, we build up our spirits and bolster our faith. Matthew 11:28–30 says, "Come unto me all ye that labor and are heavy laden, and I will give you rest. Take my yoke upon you, and learn of me; for I am meek and lowly in heart: and ye shall find rest unto your souls. For my yoke is easy, and my burden is light." Jesus will give us rest and take the burden of worry away from us. Though we make plans for the future, we need not worry about tomorrow. For God knows what tomorrow holds, and if we give him control, we will make it.

Then comes the hard part: making the changes that God, through his Word, has shown us we need to make. God has a plan for our lives, and if we follow that plan, we will live with peace in our hearts. In Jeremiah 1:5 (NASV), it says, "Before I formed you in the womb I knew you, and before you were born I consecrated you." The word "knew" here means "to know by seeing." God knew your personality; he placed the desires in your heart; he knew your likes and dislikes. Jeremiah 29:11 (NIV) says, "For I know the plans that I have for you, declares the Lord, plans to prosper you and not to harm you, plans to give you hope and a future." God has plans for us and wants us to live healthy and productive lives. He wants us to prosper in every way, but we have to do it his way if he is going to help us. Noah escaped the flood. Moses led the children of Israel out of Egypt. Rahab escaped the destruction of Jericho. Elijah defeated four hundred prophets of Baal at Mt. Carmel. Gideon defeated 120,000 with an army of 300. They all did it by using God's plan. We are able to do great things for God if we 1) follow God's plan, 2) do all we are humanly capable of doing, and 3) allow God to take over, and let him have control.

Don't Look Back

Haggai was a minor prophet. That does not mean his ministry was of less importance. It means he didn't write as much. Haggai's ministry lasted about three and a half months. His sole message was to rebuild the temple. In Haggai 2:9, it says, "The glory of this latter house shall be greater than of the former." I was reading that one day and paused and wondered what God meant by that statement. God said don't look back. That phrase is a reference to rebuilding the temple. The Israelites had neither the means nor the money to rebuild it in the glory and grandeur that Solomon had built it. Yet God said that the "latter house shall be greater than the former" Haggai 2:9. Maybe God is not quite as concerned with monetary things as we humans are. We should work within our means.

God is telling us that it is important to go to church. That is his ordained agency. But equally important is a personal relationship with him. If we keep that relationship open and personal with God, we might be surprised what he would do in our lives. Amos 3:7 says, "Surely the Lord does nothing unless he reveals His secret counsel to his servants the prophets." In Bible times, God only spoke to prophets, priests, and kings. In our time, he wants to speak to everyone. And he will, but we have to listen. He will not speak to everyone the same way, but we have to be still and listen.

How many times have we refused change because we've never done it that way before? God has new things in store for us, which may require us to change the way we do things. We have to be open to the Lord's leading and allow him to show us new things. God does not want us to stay in our comfort zones, because the comfort zone does not require faith. We are to walk by faith, not by what is comfortable. Faith will stretch you; faith will cause you to keep walking even when all you can see is the next step and no farther. Sometimes we spend so much time looking back at the "good old days" that we can't see what God has in store for us in the future. Sometimes we can't see the beauty that is in front of us because we are looking back at what is behind us. We can't see the future because we are too busy looking in the past. It's not wrong to reminisce about the past, but let's not set up camp there. When we do look back, we should see a progression, a series of events that leads us closer to God. We should be able to see what God has brought us through.

We can't change the past, but we can affect the future. Don't let your past take up too much of your future. In Ephesians 2:10, it says, "For we are his workmanship, created in Christ Jesus unto good works, which God hath before ordained that we should walk in them." We were created perfect by God, but sin got in the way, and since God is perfect, only perfection is good enough. Sin is not so much a crime against the law but a crime against love. We did not break the law as much as we broke God's heart. The only way to be reconciled to God is through forgiveness. We then should do the works of God out of gratitude, not out of penance or atonement for our sins. Jesus is our atonement.

Always remember that the will of God never takes you to where the grace of God will not protect you. God's plan is a perfect plan. If we follow that plan, we will have all we need to accomplish that plan. God will see us through. First John 1:9 says, "If we confess our sins, he is faithful and just to forgive us our sins, and to cleanse us from all unrighteousness." Forgiveness is ours for the asking.

Matthew 8:21 says, "Another of his disciples said unto him, Lord, suffer me first to go and bury my father." Jesus response in verse 22 was, "Follow me; and let the dead bury their dead." Jesus was not being cold and heartless here. The young man was fulfilling his duties to his family by seeing that they were taken care of. Then he would follow Jesus. We must follow Jesus now, not later when we have done what we feel is necessary—not that we should neglect family. It is scriptural to take care of them. But we must follow God first.

Several times in the New Testament, Jesus says, "Follow me." The word "follow" means "to cling to, imitate, or pursue." If we are to follow someone, we have to watch what that person does and imitate him or her. We have to do this until we get their pattern ingrained in our memory. We have to cling to that person's way of doing things. That means we may have to pursue new ways sometimes. We can't be looking back at the way we used to do it. We can't live in the past and expect to find a better way of doing things. Albert Einstein said he never came to any of his discoveries through the process of rational thinking.

It is said of Thomas Edison that he failed a thousand times before he made a light bulb that worked. When asked about failing that many times, he responded that he found a thousand ways *not* to make the light bulb.

When God brought Lot out of Sodom, he instructed him not to look back but to flee to the hills. He didn't show Lot a complete plan or a set place to run to. He just said to run and not look back.

Sometimes we need to run from our pasts. Yes, we had some good times, and we had some memorable moments. But we need to look ahead and believe that God has greater things in store for us. It's called living by faith, and that is not always easy.

By reading the Bible, we will see the character of God. He really is loving and kind. He does want what is best for us. And no, he does not want us to live in poverty so that we will be more spiritual.

If your children asked for something to eat, would you give them a stale piece of bread or a dried-out roll? If they asked for a burger, would you give them one out of the fridge that was two weeks old? Of course not—but we seem to think that's the way our heavenly Father will treat us. God wants to give us many things, but we don't let him.

Joel 2:3 says, "The land is like the garden of Eden before them, and behind them a desolate wilderness." The prophet Joel is using a devastation of locusts as an analogy of the coming end times. Let's not spend so much time looking back that we can't see the present, let alone the future. We can't change the past, but we can affect the future. Sometimes we make shambles out of our lives and think God can't use us. Good news! God can make all things new and restore us if we let him. We should learn from the past to make changes to the present that will affect the future.

Roger Derksen was driven by the Holy Spirit to write *Extreme Makeover*. He has studied the Bible for years and now writes to inspire others to do the same. Derksen lives in Kansas City with his wife of forty years, Debb. They have two children and seven grandchildren.

BIBLIOGRAPHY

Barclay, William. "Gospel of Mark." *The Daily Study Bible Series.* Philadelphia: Westminster Press, 1975.

———. "Gospel of Matthew." *The Daily Study Bible Series.* Philadelphia: Westminster Press, 1975.

Gordon, Lindsay. *Prayer That Moves Mountains.* Dallas: Christ for the Nations, 1998.

Hagin, Kenneth E. *The Art of Prayer.* RHEMA Bible Church, Tulsa, OK 1992.

Hart, Archibald D. *Thrilled to Death.* Nashville: Thomas Nelson, 2007.

Noonan, David. *Aesop and the CEO.* Nashville: Thomas Nelson, 2005.